SELECTED POEMS

JAMIE McKENDRICK

Selected Poems

---

ff

FABER & FABER

First published in 2016
by Faber & Faber Ltd
Bloomsbury House
74–77 Great Russell Street
London WC1B 3DA

Typeset by RefineCatch Limited, Bungay, Suffolk
Printed by Martins the Printers, Berwick-upon-Tweed

A CIP record for this book
is available from the British Library

ISBN 978–0–571–32729–4

2 4 6 8 10 9 7 5 3 1

Contents

from OUT THERE (2012)

SELECTED POEMS

from
THE SIROCCO ROOM

&

A born rebel, at ease in your outrage
you refuse the armchair's invitation
to slump in a heap or sleep in a hump.

I'm by contrast on a hardbacked chair
sitting prim and tightarsed as Britannia
with a shield of books and a chewed biro.

The argument we're having is unravelling
the ends that look so odd now
they're asunder, we can only wonder

how they ever did get joined together.
It seems we've unwound an ampersand and
pulled it like a cracker. On the third chair

the black-and-white cat and the white-and-black,
love-locked in a tricky double helix,
keep licking each other's necks.

Cornbride

The cornfield
is a gold comb
or a sunned fleece
the wind grooms

to a shadow
or perhaps a cloud
the wind kites
is trailing shadow

miles behind
as a bride trails
broad muslin veils
in daylight outside

though already
she's being led
with a light tread
along the aisle.

from Lost Cities

A Lost City

Heaven is the country of the exiles.
They travelled here for refuge or for rest,
To learn the language or to taste the fruit.
Years pass. A cloud occludes the mountain's foot
And the road home is overgrown with mist,
The white edges of a virgin forest
Neither daytrip nor exodus defiles.

The bread is good and bitter but still leaves
The palate aching for an absent flavour.
The shopping malls have windows where you find
Instead of your own face, a heedful neighbour
Whose joy to find you may be just as feigned.
Is your face too so transfigured and tanned?
Less old each day, less coarsened by beliefs?

Perhaps this isn't heaven after all.
The walls are veined with rose and polished beryl
– An ichor that you don't know how to tap.
New arrivals are treated with such awe,
Robed in colours, in light, as if each step
They take will help us trace some lost Before
Which if it ever was we can't recall.

Decadence

It was the time of day when the soul speaks Latin
with a Gothic slur, and sees in every direction
an evening made of basil and magenta.

There was no breeze, and we were walking
by the canals and office-blocks of Carthage.
You were in a sour mood and foresaw

only war and burning, widows and orphans.
I suggested we stop at a bar for sherbet
– the latest thing, sprinkled with ginger.

From there, we could see the queen on her terrace
sporting her would-be wedding gown, its train
of damask roses twined with ears of corn.

The light took on a green tinge and a drunk
ex-mercenary kept muttering about drift-lines
where banded kraits would coil to clean their scales

– diamonds glittering in the sea-junk.
It made no sense to me, but sense
was not what I was after. I wanted dreams.

As dusk drew in its final flecks of gold
I felt the black north couching in my bones.

Margin

Some played volleyball using fishing nets;
some drank cans of Peroni; others searched
inland for flints and sources of clear water.

I wandered by the shore towards the harbour
and the blind lighthouse of Palinurus,
and found a dolphin turning at the tide's hem

bluntly, its skin fraying on the sharp stones;
then the stringy, knifed wheeze of the helmsman
came back from the shadows and a light struck

fire through the mute larynx of the rock
at Cumae – the mad woman humming just to calm him:
That cruel place will always bear your name.

Nostalgia

I woke drenched in sweat and homesick
for nowhere I could think of, a feeling
scuffed and quaint as farthings or furlongs.

Then I remembered the room of the sirocco
in a Sicilian palace made of pink volcanic sugar.
There was a scent of waxed oak and pistachios.

Two maids were making up our nuptial bed,
smoothing the white linen with their dark hands.
You'd never have finished finding fault in their work

if I hadn't intervened, so that you turned on me
saying *Their family were turnip doctors
at the time of the Bourbons* – an old enmity then,

and more imperious even than pleasure.
How to get out of that windowless room,
with not one of its walls adjoining the air

was all I could think of, from that point on.
Your voice pursued me down the marble stairway:
Don't think you'll ever find a home again!

Memory

The staff are picketing the pleasure gardens
of the Baia Hotel with placards.
The sun is trying to melt the rocks.

The Hohenzollerns and the Hohenstaufens
are having their annual conference inside
while their saffron-tinted, air-conditioned coaches

loaf in the parking lot above the cliff
and their drivers try to read the placards
– something about the bay being soiled,

a filter, and embezzled public funds.
I've got to know each curve of this coast road
as the car hairpins like a cardiograph.

(From a distance, it is gently bow-shaped.)
I know where a barn owl nests and where
the agaves leap from their rootstock toeholds

and could tell of the netted lemon groves
that hesitate on parapets so narrow
you want to talk them back to safety;

and of the watchtowers underwater,
the window where a moray eel is curled . . .
but I won't – this need to depict

is just a weakening of the hold I have
on that rockface, a fatal stepping-backwards
onto glazed blue tiles that are tiles of air.

Axle-Tree

I lurk like a stowaway in the dark threshold
of your block of flats and wait for a sign.

I park my wreck beside the lorries that slouch
at the curb till dawn, laden to the tusks
with mahogany logs from Senegal.

At the docks, just a caber's toss away,
where row after row of raw pink Fiats
are waiting for Legion to possess them,

they season in heaps and no sooner move
than they come to a halt, as if obeying
some natural imperative. Your balcony

gives on timber seeping resin
in the moonlight; the mountains bracketing
the bay's black waves as they fret

the sea-front and the frail hull
of the unfrequented *Nave-Ristorante*
moored under the cement factory's toxic plume.

It's all crammed in like a tourist's map.
Nightshifts, headlamps and the desultory tide.
The palm fronds shrugging on the promenade.

Loosed from the shaggy leggings of those logs
I expect a windfall of tree snakes and insects
to seep through the holes of my peel-back roof.

Only last week a scorpion stung you.
Starting as a fire on the side of your thigh
it came to a head in a charred violet point . . .

You became irascible and superstitious
and dreamed of a horrible martyrdom.
You felt my star-sign made me somehow to blame

as if I'd hired a familiar for the crime.
My car fell under suspicion. You began to call it
The Touring Insect House, checking the seats

and shadows on entering, where before
you'd merely likened it to the bin-skips
with their beds of decomposing ash-blue mulch.

I've my doubts too. Do lovers use it by night?
Its suspension is not what it used to be.
Beer bottles, cigarette packets with odd

brand-names, chewed gum-wads: all add up to something
– nocturnal depredations! Anything could live there
biodegrading, unobserved, while the rear-view mirror

makes headlights flare like stars snapped out of fixity
and the hewn trunks seem lengths of a broken axle
around which once the leaf-green planet turned.

De-signifiers

Rust and dry rot and the small-jawed moth
are our best friends and they wish us well,
undoing the fabric of our heaven.

They correspond to something inside us
that doesn't love the works our hands have made
– wire-cutters, pick-locks, saboteurs.

'Are you building a good memory to have of me?'
you once asked as though I'd just begun
a papier-mâché Taj Mahal.

I keep a cardboard box of newspapers
in the cupboard so everything that's happened
is safe from pulp mills and the record-shredders

but all the while in the dark the silverfish
and woodlice are at work on the word,
its dot matrix. Living on what seems to us

dust, they profit directly from our negligence
and attention in general only provokes
their swerving, averting or curling-up manoeuvres.

Meaning? They roll it away and break it down
into unrecombinable fragments
like fatigue in our metal or cancer in concrete.

Il Capitano

He keeps a dark shed by the beach-huts and boat-houses
smelling of diesel and damp wool;
there's a yellowed notice tacked to the door
in a strange hand, or a strange tongue like the babble
of waves on pebbles, cursives of broken shell.

Bound in his nets and tackle, he carries a trident
to tap the ground in the tireless pacing
that keeps him always in sight of the sea
where the spiny rocks sift back the waves
like krill-less drizzle from the teeth of whales.

The villagers tell how once, years back,
he commanded a vessel wrecked miles out
and drifted days on a fragment of deck.
Ever since his rescue he's lived like the last man alive
in this coast resort buzzing with tourists and Vespas.

He was washed up here like the rest of us
by seed, tide, trade or fate but clearly lives,
oblivious of custom, under a different sky
– the stars urgent and legible; the miles of black salt
crashing into coves, his intimate blueprint.

It's said that sometimes he sights a ship
far out in the blue and foams with an exquisite
panic of recognition. Dropping his stick
he thrashes through the waves like a fierce child
till the fishermen gently drag him back again.

Sign Language

The deaf-mute fisherman sits in his beached boat
with the net he's mending looped round both big toes
and his left-hand thumb while his right hand weaves
in and out. Air and water crash in soundless waves
through the spaces where his livelihood will catch,
the fishes whose new names I'm slowly learning:
merluzzo, alice, dentice, pesce spada . . .
Seeing me reading, he signs that books are better
– what he earns in a day I spend in an hour
eating fish at the restaurant he supplies.

Motorini swarm in from the cities
of the plain, from the little badlands
under the shadow of Vesuvius. Then when the bars
are closed, the cars in the car park rock like boats,
their windows taped with *Il Mattino* or *L'Unità*
and I see him picking his way home
through the refuse of a beach culture
with nothing but a bemused welcoming smile
– though when he stops outside his door I'd swear
he's talking to himself with his fluent hands.

Darkness in the Mezzogiorno

Rubbish clots the courtyard's fountain sculpture
of Neptune clouting a triton with a fishbone.
There's a smell of rotting cuttlefish
off the cobbles, and an iridescent sludge
of rosy scales and silver fishes' eyes. The sea
is everywhere, and nowhere visible, like God.
It sweats through the walls where sand from the sea
was used four centuries ago for stucco.
These alleys where the local kings and *pezzi grossi*
hung out from verdant balconies
are still rich as any royal family
in the underwater categories of crime,
and seethe with bullet-headed shoals
of *ruffiani, spacciatori, camorristi.*
In winter the prostitutes sit warming
their slack calves over a fire of fruit crates.
A lack of expectation lights
along the false blonde's unbruised olive eyes.
Everything that happens happens on the streets
or overlooking them. There's no elbow-room
under the sign AREA DI MANOVRA:
for the old men playing *scopa* where
the pavement ought to be; for cars
that back up the way they came or
airwaves jammed with radios and rows;
no room to retreat where history
has made a fig-sign at the private life.
Lost empires jostle in the cellarage
and layer after layer of colonists lie shelved
under the cobbles with their dialects
and utensils – Roman, Saracen and Spaniard –

their rubbish and their triumphs petrified:
jewel-hilted daggers and medical tracts
rhymed in Latin; lacquered fans and vessels carved
for Christendom by Arab ebonists . . .
Down there are knots that no one can undo –
wounds, fingerprints and pomegranate seeds,
bedheads and olivestones and shoulderblades
in sheets of salt hid from the light of day.

from
THE KIOSK ON THE BRINK

Under the Volcano

Between the Devil's Viaduct and the deep blue sea,
any darkened patch or nook will do,
they gather for the rites of youth
– a soluble nectar that arrives
from nowhere, like a boat in the port.

Incendi dolosi. A bronze light worries
the night sky where the hillside
consumes itself. Those
wanting compensation tie
a burning brand to a trapped bird's foot

so where the bird alights in terror
flames spread. No one's
the wiser as when the camorra
firebomb a discotheque or bar.
You sense the sulphur under the earth's crust

The cortège follows the boy
they found in the Park of Springtime,
his forearm dandling a syringe.
Between the viaduct and the seafront
you crush the brittle flowers underfoot.

The Vulcanologist

Athanasius   Kircher
having   completed   his
key work on Coptic grammar
(and rightly linked it to the
hieroglyphs)   left   the   cardinals
in Rome and set about his Latin tract
on volcanoes. He visited Etna and Vesuvius,
and Vesuvius he entered, let down the inner
walls by lengths of rope, growing smaller and
smaller like a bug on a thread tacked to the sky's
vault with tiny pins of adamant. There he swung past
fumaroles with poison yellow plumes, abseiling through
gardens of brimstone and red cinders. He saw the vestibule
he knew would lead to a vast network of subterranean flames,
lakes of bitumen and burning conduits threading land and ocean
from Iceland to Patagonia. In his book he mapped fire's empire and
its outposts, the whole racked body of Hephaestos, whose molten heart
we build our spindly cities on, and plant and tend our perishable groves

Ye Who Enter In

after Antonio Machado

To plumb the depths of hell and meet
ministers, saladins and scholars,
Marilyn Monroe and Cleopatra,
the latter naked as the day they died;
to give audience where you please
and where you don't to curl your lip
or deftly rabbit-punch a kidney,
sure that your arm is power-assisted.
To be steered about by someone who just
happens to be Virgil, and you like his poems.
To write as a chisel writes on rock
so every phrase you write resounds forever:
ABANDON ALL HOPE . . . You first.
No really I insist please after you.

Sky Nails

That first day, to break me in,
my hardened comrades
sent me scampering like a marmoset
from the topmost parapet

to the foreman's hut
for a bag of sky nails.
The foreman wondered which precise
shade of blue I had in mind.

It's still sky nails I need today
with their faint threads
and unbreakable heads

that will nail anything
to nothing
and make it stay.

The Seismographical Survey

Crumbling the tarmac into treacly clods
tufts of weed were using their green levers
on the disused airfield we drove across
to load our jeep up from the magazine
– that padlocked booth among the bulrushes
stacked with boxes of waxed cardboard sticks
and fuses trailing nervous wires . . .
We'd start where yesterday's fresh boreholes
lipped with screws of clay
made ten-yard strides across Derbyshire
then stop beside each hole and blow it up.
I tamped the 1 lb stick of dynamite
with a nine-foot copper-ended pole
and fixed the fuse-wires to the detonator
which Arthur plunged so that the thump and spray
would surface as a heartbeat on the graph
in the technician's van which followed us
dark-windowed, white, a kind of ambulance.
And casualties occurred
though they were after something under us;
I never found out whether coal or oil
but Arthur's guess was that they found fuck all.
Day after day we'd trample through and cancel
field after field of corn rape barley pasture
and the odd head-high field of sunflowers
and in our wake we sowed a line of craters
and echoes beaking down through soil and bedrock
and sods and divots falling in slow motion.

The last day we bumped into this farmer
sleepily trudging through a field of his
balancing two offcuts of one coathanger
bent into right angles.

After we'd shed our loaded shoulderbags
he showed us how to hold those L-shaped wires
lightly, how they made an X
above the water-channels we took on trust
then gradually uncrossed as we walked on
and how this other way with our own hands
we answered to those echoes underground.

Et In Orcadia Ego

Having heard the Orkneys were like Eden
we sold up everything and bought a farm.
A subsistence farm, I called it. There wasn't sun
enough for solar panels – the rays fell
at such an oblique angle, it was clear
they were heading for somewhere else,
some kinder place with trees. All round the year
the big winds tore about with wasteful power.
I felt that just by being there
I was tilting at windmills. Did I have to
build them as well? Since then I've often thought
if we'd run the water-pipes beneath the henshit
like smoky lava on the floor of the coop
we could have had hot water winterlong.

The last straw was a goat-breeding project.
Hoping the meat might sell, I'd bought
this Anglo-Nubian billy to beget
a nation and populate our land. I left him
tethered to a mulberry shrub . . . when God
stumbled upon the body of Abel
in the murderous quiet of the day
and sent Cain off to chew the bitter cud
he must have felt as I felt in that empty place.
The farm pony was looking darkly innocent
and the kid had withdrawn into his yellow gaze
– the colour made me think of Nile mud –
his jaw stove in by the pony's hoof.
All attempts to heal or tend him failed
and, though neither I nor Anne could keep it down,
we ended eating our last chance to stay.

The Agave

also called aloe, maguey, the century plant,
only seems to flourish where
an inch would launch it into space

on cliffs and ledges and descents
beside the prickly pears that crouch
in their hairsuits like luscious grudges.

Saw-toothed, sword-shaped, its fleshy leaves
are carved with hearts and hard-ons
by agile Orlandos.

After twenty, sometimes thirty years,
out of the powerhouse of its rootstock
from which the Aztecs brewed

their pulque and clear-eyed mescal,
it sprouts a lone stem limbed with bright
unbelliferous panicles

twenty, sometimes thirty foot tall
and at a rakish angle to the rock
then dies to leave the coastline

studded with the charred masts
and gutted decks of an armada.

Tinnitus

The rustle of foil, a tide of pins, a wave
which never breaking
crinkles from the far side of the brink

and inches nearer with its crest
of decibels and wreckage under which
still you catch the cars diminishing, phrase

after phrase of the evening bird
fainter each time but holding out
from a twig upon a tree within a wood.

Terminus

Io ero tra color che son sospesi

Hanging on the hours like heliotropes
we have taken root where we set foot;
the sun favours our recreations
and salt in the seawind glazes us over
with a tan, a patina, taken for health.

We greet each other with averted eyes
and shipwrecked smiles. Otherwise
indulge in the stern vice of vivisection
and self-portraiture: exiles who left
for no reason with no reason to return.

Mountain

Ledge

The mountain would have crashed on top of us
but it needed to unlace its concrete stays
and the wire mesh that caged its overhang.

Lilies splashed with fire from the underworld
grew in a niche beneath the barn owl's nest
– all night we heard her catastrophic wheezing

and the even breathing of the tideless sea
down where the steps expired, tired of counting,
of footsoles, heels, of having to be steps

so far below while up above as far
the coast road curled and shed its cast-offs
for the morning on the balcony:

a ripe fig, a hairclip, a fag-end, a feather
and a faint premonitory sprinkling of stones.

On the Volcano

For years in the shadow of the mountain
we'd never thought to cast our shadows on it,
to peep down into it from up above . . .

Slag and clinkers; an afterthought that still
plagues the earth about her final form;
a verruca; a welt; a peak of hell

erected in the midst of paradise.
Fumes idled up the inner walls
as we stopped at the kiosk on the brink

vending cans of molten sugar, dreadful trade,
then wound back down by the parched red track
to the car park where the gypsy woman sat

with those chunks of pyrite, fool's gold, fire
cooled, cast and cubed in the dire forge.

Flood

The mountain dug its heels into the draff
that ran from its sides in ropes of gravel
as the black pearls of rain hit off the rock.

Then the sea moved in to meet the mountain's flow
and overstepped the concrete mole and wrecked
the beach-huts, the football pitch, the sandwich stall

and scaled the doorsteps and the windowsills
where it came to rest. Along that level
the bay and the square were a seamless cope

the tops of the tallest cars kept just above
while their owners circled them in rowboats
and, half its height, the square's one palm tree

rode the ripples through that inland sea
with the air of a battered periscope.

Il Tremoto

Inside the mountain earth begins to move
its joints and spring the links that pegged it down
– the fans of schist, the chocks and wedges of

feldspar and chert. A daylight owl screws back
from rock that spilling derelicts her nest
then quiet plugs the ear, a twist of wax.

Behind the quiet a core of silence hums
until earth moves again – this time in earnest:
dumb matter's rigid-tongued delirium

wrung at the verge of the crack that gapes at
the heart of things, that widens the Norman watchtower
from its sunken gateway to the parapet

as the tide uncoils. This means in purgatory
a soul pinned to the rock has broken free

Lengths of Air

The mountain had its shoulders in the cloud
it kept its head above, rich folds of cloud
with tassels spilling round a clump of rock.

Above the cloud a village like a wasps' nest
in fractured soapy pinks and crusted honey
hung on to nothing by a thread

and from its topmost balcony a woman
let out the rope that let her basket down
past the cloud, the winding road, the lemon groves

in their black nets and down the mountainside
until it reached sea-level where I knelt
and found inside the photo and the note.

I trembled at that nakedness and read:
here I am on my bed inlaid with lapis.

Hortus Conclusus

The Reptilarium has parked under the palm tree
like an Ark on wheels, a seething caravan
it costs no more than the news to enter.

Tomorrow we can read about the world
but today we'll wander back to origin
and see through glass what took Eve's breath away

and gave it back quickened. The sleepy snakes
lie wreathed around themselves or slither through
the hoops of their own skin, their hanks of hemp.

A tongue or a mouse's tail retracts within
the lipless smile of a green tree python.
Such heavy necklaces! So far from Eden!

The driver counts the coins into his tin.
The sun curls its last rays round the mountain.

Sirensong

Why do you think he went on wandering
after the orchestrated pathos of his homecoming
– the hot bath, the clean sheets, the postal code?

It wasn't that he was bored by his wife;
more she by him and by those years of waiting
(for what?) with better prospects close at hand.

It wasn't as he pretended the desire
to travel to the edge of the known world
where he could found some godforsaken waste.

Lashed to the mast, did he think the wax
he'd also plugged his own ears with would work?
And that the siren's downcast eyes expressed

the fear she'd lost him not the lack of doubt
her voice would carry till it found him out?

Skin Deep

The headlamps of divers
cast a greasy cloud of light just under
the sea's dark skin. Before you can blink

the octopus has played a symphony
of russet stipples and black bands
across its back. It thinks in colour.

Beware and welcome have twenty inflections
like Delacroix saying Mon cher monsieur
– for tomorrow's lunch they'll all boil down

to an inky sauce, some Redon lithograph
of spiders dancing in the afterlife.

Stood Up

The clock turns bulbous, fish-eyed, whiskery.
The longlegged clock-hands take scissory strides
above you. Darts spring back from the jumbled dial,
pointedly snubbed, while you still wait

for a breathless explanation that would lift,
as a seal lifts a beachball, the dead weight
of your chin, of the hours, propped on your arm's
Dalì stilt now that the clock has melted

in pools of spilt beer islanding the ashtray
and only the wind judders the swingdoors
or else some stranger. Half-stewed, old droopy-jaws

who winds the grizzled ends of his moustache
might well be you, but ten years on, still waiting
for love to walk in before closing time.

from
THE MARBLE FLY

Ancient History

The year began with baleful auguries:
comets, eclipses, tremors, forest fires,
the waves lethargic under a coat of pitch
the length of the coastline. And a cow spoke,
which happened last year too, although last year
no one believed cows spoke. Worse was to come.
There was a bloody rain of lumps of meat
which flocks of gulls snatched in mid-air
while what they missed fell to the ground
where it lay for days without festering.
Then a wind tore up a forest of holm oaks
and jackdaws pecked the eyes from sheep.
Officials construing the Sibylline books
told of helmeted aliens occupying
the crossroads, and high places of the city.
Blood might be shed. Avoid, they warned,
factions and in-fights. The tribunes claimed
this was the usual con-trick
trumped up to stonewall the new law
about to be passed. Violence was only curbed
by belief in a rumour that the tribes
to the east had joined forces and forged
weapons deadlier than the world has seen
and that even then the hooves of their scouts
had been heard in the southern hills.
The year ended fraught with the fear of war.
Next year began with baleful auguries.

Vehicle

I jolt awake at the wheel of this wreck
made of resin, crystals and cracked amber,
its dashboard dial a compass pointing south.

All the things I ever had and kept –
old files, old coats and age-old daily papers,
smudged and piss-yellow, fly out the rear window

unravelling and tearing in the backdraught
and snagging on the dark umbrella pines
that line the coast now that the rocks have turned

to the sand we glimpse when the wood gives way
to trees. The mozzarella buffalo are chewing
lumps of earth and barely lift their heavy heads

to watch us. The hard shoulder's a fur-rack
of flattened stoats and moles and the odd dog
lying among pools of oil and shattered bodywork.

We pass the dead city with its four gates,
three temples and twice-flowering roses;
then the one stall selling painted urns and postcards.

A black-haired woman stands by the road
in a tight lowcut black crape dress –
for miles the wind brings lovely skeins and pockets of

her spikenard perfume through the former windscreen
with flakes of darkness which we wipe away
like ash-filled cobwebs or swart veils of lace.

And as the sun drops to the lacquered sea
it's hard to figure out how long the car
can hold together, given the speed it's going,

[44]

or how long it's been since we set out
trailing tiny shining cubes of glass
and scattering scraps of everything I've owned

past so many earthworks and abandoned
homes that now it seems I'm staring
out at the Pole Star through a window of bone.

A Roman Ruin

RIP Wolseley 1500, MOT
failure cum laude, rust-plaqued, cough-racked jade,
eyesore, ossiary, tin tub, dustbin
– that last oil can was your extreme unction.

What's left can be my memento mori
or a monument to Britain's now decayed
industrial base. There's a sepia postcard
bluetacked to your walnut dashboard

of the ruined palace of one Septimus
– weeds feasting off its arches much as moss
(some rolling stone) does on your window rim.

O pilgrim, you who search for Rome in Rome . . .
Forget it. Neither the Tiber nor the Thames
will be graced again by your ancient chrome.

The Spleen Factory
after Carlos Drummond de Andrade

I want to make a sonnet that's not a sonnet
according to any civilised notion of what
that is. I want it ugly as concrete,
and just about impossible to read.

And I'd like my sonnet in the future
to give no living soul an ounce of pleasure,
not by being merely foulmouthed and perverse
but also (why not?) by being both and worse

if it feels the urge. Plus I want the whole thing caustic
and obtrusive – with intent to pierce and hurt
like stitches done without anaesthetic

somewhere tender. So it won't be learnt by heart.
So it's a wall with a hole pissed through – in the hole a star
transmitting incomprehensible clarity.

The One-Star
for Michael Hofmann

Moving away in the taxi, I could just see myself
    climbing the marble steps and stepping through
    the plate glass into a lounge-cum-vestibule,

its floor inlaid with a pink star of mineral grains
    and roughage – a breakfast for the afterlife.
    Beaded oak cladding, electrified oil lamps,

a pharaonic desk clerk. The air was cut and dried
    as though reconstituted in the basement's lungs
    and laid out, and folded, in cool dry reams.

The Shining was obtainable on the video service
    but would be scrambled after several minutes
    if you failed to press the 'Confirm' button

– otherwise it was a sex film I was embarrassed
    for the glamorous Thai receptionist
    to know I was watching. So I tried to read

The Temptation to Exist feeling conspicuously
    absent and uneasily aware
    of being ironed flat, flatter, by the clean sheets

and of the bedside table's inbuilt clock
    with its defective digits: every minute
    was a minus sign or a gnomon, every hour

was missing a slant side to its parallelogram.
    I closed the eyelids of the two nightlights;
    then mine . . . until I woke as though I'd feasted

on finely ground enamel. There was nothing for it
    but to go home – some home! – but first why not
    spirit away the bar of opalescent soap, the small

urn of bath-foam and the shroud-sewing kit
   the size of a matchbook, with loops of thread
   five different shades of grey

or maybe it was the light? I had a good mind
   to mend the inside lining of my coat
   but instead went down in the shiny lift

and sank in an armchair by the crystal ashtray.
   Was I a Mr John Ashbery, someone asked me.
   No, I replied, not Mr Ashbery

– but pausing mysteriously mid-sentence as I felt
   he deserved a couple more guesses for being
   somehow on the right track, if not exactly warm.

The pause obviously disturbed him. He didn't
   like that pause. Well tell him
   if you'd be so kind that his taxi's waiting.

Oh yes I could just see myself doing that.

The Marble Fly

The guide crinkled his nose
like a squirrel with a nut
as he pointed out to us
the baked-clay phallus
on the oven door, no doubt
symbolic of the risen loaf.

Red dust and stone thresholds
to an unrecovered world,
stone fruit that Felix
the fruitseller sold, stone-cold
drinks from the hot drinks stall,
wheel ruts cut in the stone road.

Murals, mosaics, mysteries:
the pierced stag, the girl's back
exposed to the beaded whip,
a lion mauling the shift of Thisbe
whilst a wall-eyed Pyramus
has severed an artery.

A wall relief in the Wool Market
shows the animal world in marble
– a lizard can-opening a cricket,
a mouse airlifted by an owl
and a fly (watch out, fly!)
on its own among the bulrushes –

all perfectly preserved and just
a shade larger than lifesize
and much stiller than life and harder.
It can't have been long after
that much the same idea
occurred to Vesuvius.

Span

Eye-level with the alps of ash and slag
I trawl my floor for a BT counterfoil
deep into its scarlet monitory phase
through shards and rags and scraps
and rivelled gold tobacco threads and these
long white hairs which must be mine
alas as no one else
would venture into this rented room
except one short-haired black-haired cat.
And here's a flea he carried on his back,
a tiny emissary from the caliphat
of bad dreams, doing vaults and back-flips
onto three golden dusters, bought last year
and still sealed in polythene,
their hems blanket-stitched with crimson thread
in a series of small 'v's overlapping
the dictionary. Crimson: it burns a fuse
the length of a dusty trail of roots
back to Arabic: qirmizi:
meaning the scarlet grain insect which breeds
on the kermes oak – stuff Solomon hung
beneath the wrought-gold
five-cubit wingspan of the cherubim . . .
Crimson lights up back along the line of
the trade-routes west, at each camel-stop
or port – a vowel-shift, a letter
dislodged from the throat to the palate
colouring the sound. My eyes lift
to the level of the window, facing east
onto brickwork, tarmac and slate tiles.
Upon the windowsill – a fly's black torso,
deep in the mire of last year's dust,

with its seraph wings still poised for flight
but cumbersome like panes
of leaded glass or paddles of cracked quartz,
tired for a while of beating at the air.

The Duet

From the eaves of the room I live in
comes a din as parliamentary and relentless
as windscreen wipers on a dry windscreen
– tremulous ballads to domestic bliss
which rarely get beyond the first failed line.
But then the clatter of my electric Canon,
its pinhead headbutting the daisywheel,
will stop them gargling gravel for a while.

It's at it again, their silence might be saying,
it's nature's joke the way those creatures sing.
And, as hardly ever, if it should go on
over the page an indignant pigeon,
that's my excuse, rakes the gutter with its claws
and creaks into flight like a rusty hinge.

Flight

for Valerie Lipman

spruce hickory bamboo
(though only for a few seconds)
the first aircraft flew

as if the wind had a mind
to clear the air of any weather
that might tilt the scales
one way or the other

as the tenons quaked
and the dowelling screaked
and the single rear rudder

came to grief
like the tail
or tailfeather
of an unfledged hippogriff.

In the Hold

Route-marching, field-postcards, tents hung with scrim
– we waited in those Domesday parishes
for D-Day to begin.

Beyond the wood there was a flint-harled church
and a watertower like a missile in plainclothes
– a tall tube with a concrete hat on top.

I can still feel the pink rim the beret left
embossed on my receded hairline
and the veins in my forehead swelling

with the notes of the bird I couldn't see
bubbling like water through a sea-vent
while darkness linked the leaves and thickened.

From Suffolk they drove us down by night
to the New Forest where we were nearer still
the zero-hour

that months of training had prepared us for
not thinking too far ahead of or about
by filling the days with strict inspections.

And then the lorry drive in convoy
to the blunt-hulled landing ships,
the gangplank a small step from the footboard.

Once in the hold I heard the air compress
as the round steel hatch was clamped down shut
and tightened by a half-turn on the hand-grips

and there we all were in the dim light that came on
stowed in the hollow belly of the war
– a box that clanged and stank of diesel –

till daylight heaped us on the other shore.

Ultima Thule

On a family outing to the final island,
wobblingly tall, the fools of ocean, together
we rode the rubber dinghy. Our father manned

the stunted paddles, blade on the feather,
regardless of the waves chilled from world's end.
The black hexagonal basalt columns reared

like a row of crayons worn down at different
rates from scribbling on the ether,
the nearest – pedestals for cormorants.

Like weathervanes, the rowlocks slithered round.
The boat floor pumped and tussled like a heart
sculpting our insteps with its upthrust as

the island rowed itself away from us,
towering at the edge of time forever.

Taken Awares

I fall into every trap
they set for me –
mantrap, mousetrap, birdlime.

Every time
I take the bait –
the worm, the cheese, whatever.

I pluck the wire
that shifts the lever
that springs the teeth.

Then, in the calm before death,
I flatter myself
I'd seen it all a mile off.

I even manage a small laugh.

Six Characters in Search of Something

A friend of mine met the son of a man
who it seems was eaten by a polar bear
in Iceland where the bear had stepped ashore
rafted from Greenland on an ice-floe.

The father of the man who met my friend
saw the bear who'd eat him loitering near
the shore and hurried on and met another man
who was walking the other way towards the bear.

He gave that other man his walking stick
but the bear meanwhile had doubled back
and reappeared on the path ahead
of the man who now was unprotected.

There may be a moral in this story
for the man, his son, the man he met,
for my friend, for me, or even for the bear,
but if there is it's better left unsaid.

Name-Tag

Every sock and collar has a name-tag.
I have a name, a surname, and a tartan rug
with tassels. What else? A zip-up
pigskin letter-writing case that's pitted
where the bristles have been scorched away.
Once a week we write neat letters home with
our marks and team scores which the master reads.
Mornings, we get a tick for shitting
after the prefect has inspected it.
Through the keyhole old MacMillan
is sitting on his single bed
and talking to the service revolver
he uses with blanks to start the races.
Our toes are fat red bulbs from chilblains.
Already one skin has rubbed away, another grown
harder than the first, a kind of pigskin.
We must never sneak or blub or suck up.
We wear steel studs that spark. Scoured lugs
stick out from crew cuts as we learn by heart
the Latin for pitching camp and waging war
and the psalm where I am made
to lie down in green pastures and a table
is prepared for me and my enemies.
The tables are mopped with swab rags,
the dustbins tipped among the ferns
and bamboo of the watergarden
for this was once a country house
and we are lucky to enjoy the fine grounds
which we see through the barred windows
or on Sunday walks trying to keep up
with the master who ran the marathon.

In the wooden locker by the metal bed
I have a chipped enamel mug,
a toothbrush, a comb, a nailbrush and two shoebrushes
with which, with time, I could scrub away
my shoes, my nails, my hair, my teeth –
given time enough, the buildings, the pitches,
the gate's ironwork with its clawing lion
and all we've learnt till nothing's left
but the Blasted Oak I carved my name on
and perhaps the derelict pavilion.

Gainful Employment

As if I had nothing better to do,
and who says I have, than putting the house
I haven't got in order, I sit at the oak desk
I have got, though really a table not a desk
but it's mine and I sanded it down myself
and beeswaxed it with iron wire-wool

– that was how important it was for me:
this surface on which so much was to be
accomplished. Best of all, I can take
its legs off, and replace them by way of
four angelic wing-nuts to the corner brackets
so it's both a steadfast and a movable beast.

But I wonder why I kept this biro spring
I'm exercising now between my finger
and thumb – not to sew my eyelids up with
like the envious spirits in purgatory.
Just too exquisite to throw away,
an image of infinity or information . . .

I'm still here, where there's an unconsolable
joy to be had, sitting ready at my station
and waiting for the bugle or the slughorn.
No one can say it's wasting time, my time, the time I've got,
to enter the very thread of the helix,
to live always expecting the unheard of.

Possession

This patch of green attached to the rented house
belongs to the clutches of the ivy
I've begun (what's got into me?)
to rip from the sycamore trunk it's clamped on
and from the lawn where its cables,
like supply lines, are dug in
through bronchial roots, and bear an iron code:
extend, secure. It tears the skin from my fingers,
expressing a thin milk, probably poison.
In one afternoon, I've undone seasons
of reinforcement, of slow dominion
as though I had a new law to dispense.

As though I had some hanging gardens in mind.
But the verminous life-forms it's helped
advance: spiders, woodlice and snails that creep,
at their respective paces, back and away
in search of cover. The earth itself
seems dank and affronted, and a death's-head moth
foxes my eyelids like a page of Euclid
– all painted dust, bristling and admonitory.
Soon enough I'll be tangled up like Laocoön
on the compost heap, my wrists and ankles bound,
and the small creatures will be at home in me
and my mouth will sprout a glossy angular leaf.

A Shortened History in Pictures

The Child Maximilian in a White Frock.
The Imperial Family with their Chairs and Pet Cat.
Maximilian, a Thoughtful Young Man in Black.
Maximilian, Emperor of Mexico, at Court.
The Empress of Mexico, his Wife Charlotte.
The Emperor Maximilian on Horseback.
Maximilian and his Court Playing Cricket
(with the English Ambassador, Sir Charles Wyke).

The Broken Cacti and the Convent's Outer Wall.
The Execution Squad Standing to Attention.
A Campesino Leading a Llama under Popocatépetl.
The Execution of Miramón, Mejía and Maximilian.
The Gold-Green Tail-Feathers of the Quetzal.
The Emperor's Shirt after his Execution.

Gardener's World

Yes, we're in the potting-shed again this week
with Mr Jones among the seedlings . . .
his wrinkles have dug in, his intellectual fingers
are a dark pollen-coated mothy umber.
He's in, he's always in, his overcoat
which when he moves gives off a sweetened cloud
of twine and potash like a hardware store.

The owners of the garden where he works
have kept a special mug for his own use
called Jonesies Mug, though no one else
would dream of using it. He sips the tea,
the florid healthy colour of flowerpots,
while muttering to the calyx of a small tomato:
Well, the Missis is a bit under the weather today.

– A figure of speech that falls a fraction short.
Right now she's barricading their front door
with thousands of cans of catfood
she'd stockpiled in the cellar against
the years of famine. He shrugs and walks away
like a dazed tortoise in the stiff panels
of his coat then stoops into the boiler-house

which stores his various implements besides
an unexplained medicine-ball like a prize pumpkin.
His cup of tea has turned as cold as stone.
And now he's ambled way beyond the rockery.
And now he's gone – the cracked furry boots
and the creases of his pass-the-parcel face
are lost forever out among the lupins.

On/Off

The switch stuck through the lampstand's neck
like an arrow shaft of walrus ivory
in a Welsh epic
has lost its feathers and its head.
Peacock feathers and a gold head.
Its Fiat Lux
with a length of flex,
its shift, its crick has made me
blink like a lemur at the lack
of the moon or a star
or a thing between. But it's good
how someone takes off their earrings
with the motion of shelling a pea.
A tiny snap. Like the hasp-click
of a calyx
at the press of a picker's thumb.
A sound like lifting an airtight lid
or a pin dropping in a pyramid.
Then the lobe's set free
and breathes with delight
to shed the slight weight
of the earrings.
Earrings that might be
twin filaments, a pair of ball-bearings
or a hammock-faced moon and a tarnished star.

Legacies

It was in the cellar of the Edinburgh house
owned by my great great grandfather

that the bodysnatchers, Burke & Hare,
unknown to him, kept their cache of corpses

in cold storage before delivering them
to the School of Human Anatomy.

There was always a skeleton in the closet,
or a skull at least, perched among the army berets,

the Luger, the greatcoat, the Zeiss binoculars
and the fox stole with its red glass eyes

and blackened lips which fastened with a snap.
There was always the skull in the clothes cupboard

with a fidgety script on its fontanelle,
saying nothing, its eyes reduced to zeroes.

*

In today's newspaper I read of a Xhosa chief
who believed his great great uncle's skull was kept

somewhere in Scotland. After leaving several
military museums empty-handed,

he had a dream of a field and a white horse
grazing. In the field a barn, in the barn

that skull. And there it seems he found it
– on a shelf among some tarnished bridles –

identified by a bullet hole in the temple
from a British rifle. So some day soon

may we now expect a visit from a man
with or without a leopardskin and flywhisk

who has travelled across two continents to ask
what we've kept all this time in our closet?

Galatea and Polyphemus
after Ovid

I think of the sheer foulness of Polyphemus
and then of the face of Acis which seems
unfair, it's so flawless. I lay all day
in his arms on a high green sheltered ledge
hidden from the Cyclops, that one horrid eye
molten with inflammation and fixated
on my image. I hate to think of my image
pinned down in each of his pitifully few
brain cells like a doll madonna stuck
in some wall shrine lit by a grey-pink bulb
on an alley of rats and gore and filth.
His outside's bad enough – hard ulcerated
slime a loathsome cindery mauve, his one eye
like an anus, a blob, a fronded jellyfish.
Then we heard him coming and watched him squat
on a jagged promontory, the waves matting
the pelt on his calves. He sets down that stick
tall as a ship's mast and starts puffing
at a pipe of giant reeds like a church organ.
I remember his song which went like this:

O Galatea tiny-featured as a chaffinch,
supple and slender as a rowan sapling,
smooth as Greek yogurt, as jasper beads,
silkier than the inside of an oyster
– like a secret tree in the middle of the wood
casting a violet shadow. Your breasts are
like new-made planets in the night sky
which make the stars drop from the firmament
to cluster round your feet like leaves on fire
– you fit so exactly into your skin
your small chiselled joints must be transparent . . .

[68]

I'll spare you some salacious details
of how he spied me bathing naked
– my breasts like bells of flesh, my nipples
parting the water . . . his voice all thick and hectic
though bits of his song weren't actually so bad.
That's why I remember it. I wouldn't mind
Acis pirating a few of those lines
but he more than makes up for that lack
with the lines of his profile – even his wrists,
even his callused heels are aphrodisiac
though his phrasing leaves something to be desired.
Cyclops then roughened his song with a lot of reproaches:

But, O Galatea, you're harder-hearted than gnarled oak,
falser than water, more slippery than ice,
vainer than peacocks and colder than the winter sea.
Worst of all and what I hate the most are
your sudden turns of speed in spurning me.
I'd bask in your other faults if I could just
once grab hold of you. Then see if you'd escape.
And think of all the things you're missing by not
being mine: all this mountainside, that plain
as far as those squalid dinky coast resorts
that spoil the view – I'll paste them with a layer
of mud and ash as soon as I feel myself again.
Think of the orchards bowed down with pears,
pale grapes and also black ones; my caves
uncannily tuned to body heat no matter
what season's abroad, dog days or Arctic blasts;
woodland fruits beside freshwater streams,
clumps of white-domed mushrooms, tall forests
of chestnuts, flocks of goats whose udders drip
with finest milk from which I make
clean curds by adding rennet. Are you mad?
Can't you see what I'm offering? I won't dull
your eyes with presents from the cornershop,

[69]

chocolates and daffodils – no diamanté jewels
like that cheapskate Acis gets to pin on you.
I'd dig rare gems out of the mountainside
with strange faults of fire like constellations
and fashion a necklace of dragonflies
and teach two tame owls to sing for you;
I'd twist curious lamps out of raw iron
to light you down the corridors of cave
to a bed of hoopoe crests where you would wait
for me to appear, my face dark with desire . . .
but you hate my face – it makes you cringe away.
So who says I'm that gruesome? I saw myself
in a blue pool today and thought – just look
at the size of him will you? Even Jove
who doesn't exist could never be bigger.
Does being hairy have to mean I'm vile?
Would you want a bald hound or horse, or a bird
without feathers? And if it's my one eye,
my uncompanioned eye, that bugs you what about
the sun? Two of them up there and we'd be flayed.
My eye grows on a single stem and follows
only you with its one shaft of devotion.
As for the muck on me, the stink, I'll scrub
myself with pumice every night before
we touch. Every night to touch you! O
Galatea, drop that skinny runt of an Acis
or let me at him and I'll tear his limbs
off his hairless trunk and fry them in Etna
whose channels of sulphur and blue fire
are coursing through my veins for love of you.
A love that scalds me and stops me working.
Take a look at my neglected flock. Entire fleets
pass by unscathed as if I were a lighthouse.
I just forget to wreck them. My whole life
is in arrears, in ruins like a great city

turned to burnt earth and swamps and column stumps
while all you do is quiver with disgust
at my offers and take to your exquisite heels
before I can quieten down my heartbeat
enough to speak let alone find the right words,
soft words, to let me creep closer . . .
                                                    Raucous
and needled by his own song, he stood up
and happened to spy us – the tongue of Acis
making waves through me without the use of words
when the rocks trembled with the Cyclops's cry
'That's the last you'll ever taste of love.'
I dived in the bay but my poor Acis
still crouched in a daze, he couldn't move as
Cyclops hefted up a rock and hurled it
crushing him, its edge alone sufficient
to flatten him. Blood trickled out from under
like autumn streams dyed coppery with leaf-juice
and the dense mass of rock, as though through guilt,
cracked open and a tall green reed sprang up
and waters gushed through the hollow rock
and a new youth waded out mid-stream,
his temples crowned in a wreath of rushes,
the waters round him whispering his name.

from
INK STONE

Apotheosis

His bonce high-domed like a skep, the bee-man
holds forth on how to pick a bee up by its wings
which are strong enough – it stands to reason –
to bear the weight without harm to their hinges.
As though he were a banjo player and the bee's wings
were a two-ply, fine abalone plectrum,
he demonstrates with a bumblebee on the windowframe
the exact grip between forefinger and thumb

but slips on the waxed oak floor, his arm outstretched,
neither tightening nor, regardless of his own fate,
loosening his hold on the bee one micro-notch.
I try to break his fall but move too late
for, with a dry hum, he streaks off out of reach
through the open window, still holding forth the bee.

Good Hedges

He wants the holly tree cut down to size,
the holly tree where the birds are sound, and safe
from his cat whose snickering impersonation
of birdsong – more like the din a mincer makes –
fools no one, and charms nothing out of the trees.

He wants us to tidy up the pyracantha sprouting
its fire-thorns and berry-laden fractals, and clip
the brambles, the lilacs, everything wild.
Next he'll want the hedgehog's spikes filed down,
the mole's claws bound up with green twine

– already he's replaced his own hair with ginger nylon.
His light he says is being blocked. It's dark
where he is. He has a point – so many deaths
in these few houses, it's like something
loosed from the Bible. One lucky escape, though:

the bearded roofer, one along, who lost
his footing, high on the scaffolding, and fell,
with his deck of tiles, on his shoulder and skull.
Sometimes tears come to his eyes for no reason
he can think of, but now the sun's out he sits again

on the patio, plucking from his banjo
some Appalachian strand of evergreen bluegrass,
then an Irish reel where his fingers scale
a glittering ladder like a waterfall
so even the songbirds hush in the holly tree.

Fish Eye

Hours of nothing biting on the lugworm bait
the twins had shown me how to catch – then suddenly
this spiny monster gurnard face appeared
banging about on the floor of the rowboat
like a fist or a heart. Way too scared
of its hackled gills and crest of spikes
to unthread the hook and heave it back
we froze, and watched its will to live abate
while a fog like a tide of opal stole
over the oily surface of the eye
extinguishing an eerie Borealis.
Were the cells desiccating in the iris?
Or divulging the inky depths to this new hemisphere
of air too thin, too dry and bright to bear?

Oil and Blood

Sleep on my chosen one it's only me
intent as a Madagascan sloth that moves
through the tall twilight of mahogany,
padding down the wall towards your pillowcase
and the hollows of your neck I ache for.
Lifting one knee, you shape a linen vault
that frees the scent of nard and nightflowers.
Does my dark disturb you, sweetheart, do you dream
of the rooftree burdened by a roost of bats,
your outline inscaped by their squeaky jargon?

Within a tongue's length of your ear lobe,
I could consume whole nights in this vestibule
of paradise if waiting weren't such hell
or if Van Helsing, that bony eunuch,
weren't striding upstairs with his cricket bag
full of sharpened stumps and oil of garlic,
the paraphernalia of intolerance.
Let him come. Rather than leave you be
I'd have the sun impale me and the breeze distress
my mouldy flavoured, still enamoured dust.

Right of Way

Were we expecting these toads on our doorstep?
– the smaller with a jewel stuck
to her forehead, a round white pebble,
a third eye, only blind, without a pupil,
picked up on her pilgrimage beside
the artificial lake or risking the ringroad.

It's chill and blank, that stone – perhaps a chunk
of granite ballast from the virtual quarry,
the way it seems more of an ailment
than an ornament. Her mate is clad in
eco-warrior fatigues: grey chevrons
screenprinted on a ground of dull jade.

Both have a furtive, raddled air as if
in protest at the dust fumes and the din
as the grabclaw clanks on the wagons' rim,
loading and unloading ballast. But the door open,
they make for the hallway with sagging hops
like small encrusted beanbags on the move

and seem to know, thanks all the same,
where the back door is, like it was their
house, or no house at all – their right of way
from well before we'd made such strides ahead
as building walls to live inside of, theirs before
we'd dragged our pelts and selves out of the mud.

Beyond

I spent all morning in the café talking
to a man who'd just survived a car crash.
They'd cut him out of the wreck, his legs crushed
and still not cured – his chest a map of some
forsaken country no one could live in,
as seen from the air, which was where he was then,
or felt himself to be – looking down on his own
body picked out in a ring of light though at first at least
there was no actual light there, only a dark road.
He tried to explain to me that feeling of peace
he'd had, that even now hadn't deserted him,
but did the moment when he chose (it seems a choice
was offered him) to enter his body again,
by this time in an ambulance. He became his pain,
the pain an entire horizon of hot wire,
till the paramedics pumped him full of morphine.

I told him about your accident, Lee,
the speed you were going, not forty miles per hour,
the road, the drystone wall, the service station
forecourt opposite, the date, the cloudless sky,
how the pheasant flew up from the uncut verge
into your visor or chest, as if I'd seen it,
as if I'd seen it from above or from beyond.
I listed your injuries and mentioned the man
who'd put your wristwatch, still ticking, inside
your ribbed black glove, wrapped you in a plaid rug
and dialled for help on his mobile while he kept
hold of your hand . . . I wanted to hear
how beyond the moment that has stained our lives
and left some part of us stranded on that verge,
beyond the fateful shiny insect torso of the bike
you'd been lifted up into what the man described.

In Arcana Fidei

You had a whole shelf of books devoted to death,
most of which I now have in my keeping.
God knows they're the last things I want
though till they'd passed to me I'd hardly guessed
how scrutable to some those last things are
– since then I've learnt, for instance, that
there's a smell like the smell of flowering lilac
which Swedenborg's angels use to dissuade
anyone approaching the spirit in transit.
It must find its feet first in the other world,
then – useless all denials – its deeds and crimes
are disinterred in their entirety
down to the coded entry in the diary,
the least bit of backbiting, the wronged maiden's
tearstained roundshouldered downcast look,
the poisoned cup, the stolen funds, the secret tryst . . .

Stockholm today is like the banished zone
where the lost have found their level – and me among them
after a sleepless night in the Blue Tower
where Strindberg died from a cancered gut, his mind gone
tortuous with alchemy and Swedenborg
– all round him poisoners: *a taste from hell,*
of brass and corpses. In the thin daylight here
– a narrow path between two blocks of night –
I'm free to stray from Drottninggaten's line
and chance on Swedenborg's own Minneskyrka
a small beached ark with Latin script that claims:
THE INTELLECT IS NOW PERMITTED
TO ENTER THE MYSTERIES OF FAITH

– a quaint undaunted other-worldly traffic sign
though the kirk's green spire, gilt crown and five-peaked star
make no inroads on a sky of solid cloud.

The Belen

It all seemed natural till some strange things came
and left. Butterflies eyed with pink and ochre,
a dazzling blue beneath, sauntered through the mild air

then disappeared. The river flowed both ways at once
the way a road does, but without a barrier.
It was then the bird arrived and I stopped dead

to understand it – its feathers
were the oiled russet of crushed saffron
and sown with spots that glinted like tinfoil.

Like the ruse birds have to lure a predator
away from their nest, its brief awkward flights
seemed meant to have me follow it on

through high grass right to the ends of the earth.
I wondered was this maybe some new type
of jay or hoopoe, only bigger, or

was this the bird that crossed your path and died
beside you? A woman standing on the wooden bridge
said it's just the Belen. As a doctor

she'd seen it many times before, to her
it all seemed natural but to me that bird,
which then dipped its beak and wings and tail

behind a concealed horizon in mid-air,
diving through the line of its erasure,
was as suddenly other as being born.

Singing Lessons

Barking and yepping long before I've parked,
your dog still knows the sound, the creaks and coughs
of your Citroën I've been the sole driver of
for the now exactly four years since.
It's as though she thinks one day, just once,
as the chassis sags back on its haunch of air,
it'll be your scuffed soles on the gravel walk
and then in the hall your dark asthmatic voice.
To improve which you took singing lessons – and offence
when I mimicked your teacher's fit of despair.
What stopped me then from saying that your chesty wheeze,
wrecked with Runcorn smog, Speke's pharmaceutical haze,
was always a kind of home, not just to the dog,
and as heartening as any human song?

Sea Salt

When my attention
should have been fixed
on that girl sitting there
across the table from me
after days of thinking of nothing but
or little else,
I was distracted by a crystal
she'd shed from the salt bowl
– first of all it looked
like the kind of roof a child might put
on a painted house and then more like
a see-through pyramid,
the steps of a miniature Machu Picchu
but carved from tears and not from stone.

Salt

after Montale

We don't know if tomorrow has green pastures
in mind for us to lie down in beside
the ever-youthful patter of fresh water
or if it means to plant us in some arid
outback ugly valley of the shadow
where dayspring's lost for good, interred beneath
a lifetime of mistakes. We'll maybe wake up
in foreign cities where the sun's a ghost,
a figment of itself and angular
starched consonants braid the tongue at its root
so all sense of who we are is lost to words,
and nothing that we know can be unravelled.
Even then, some vestige of the sea,
its plosive tide, its fretwork crests will surge
inside our syllables, bronze like the chant of bees.
However far we've stumbled from the source
a trace of the sea's voice will lodge in us
as the sunlight somehow still abides in
faded tufts that cling to bricks and kerbstones
on half-cleared slums or bomb-sites left unbuilt.
Then out of nowhere after years of silence
the words we used, our unobstructed accents,
will well up from the dark of childhood,
and once more on our lips we'll taste Greek salt.

The Ladder

They lean against the bedroom wall
– two equal parts of an extending ladder –
one going up, perhaps, the other down
or else the opposite. Their rungs a his-and-hers,

split-level, open-plan wardrobe handy
enough as it's worked out, without that being planned,
for grabbing clothes off. A split Jacob's ladder
for the two-way traffic of seraphim, itself an image

for DNA's double spiral peeled apart
or a sectioned Tantric spinal column showing
the downward voyage of the primal breath,
the upward urging of the spirit.

Worse days I wake to see the ladders both stop dead
like two lives shut before they reached this light,
at a white ceiling with no latch or hasp or hinge,
no up or down – a sealed floor, a solid lid.

Cataract

A half-moon is cut into the eyeball
and a liquid injected to dissolve
the protein of the lens, leaving the lens
capsule unscathed. Then – quite dark in there –
the silicone replacement is inserted
and opened up inside like an umbrella
or a ship in a bottle. When the patch
on your eye's removed
the world is full of brave new outlines,
even the angle-poised nuthatch
then the green woodpecker breakfasting
on a column of nuts is up closer,
vivider than ever, only it's all
unaccountably rose-tinted
with occasional flashes and upheavals
like a storm rolling over the Red Sea
observed by a rider on a camel.

Ink Stain

This new jacket's wrecked with an ink stain
come through from the inside breast pocket,
black with a tell-tale edge of blue-black and maroon
thanks to a leaking gadget
patented by László Bíró, the Hungarian,
and packaged by the Frenchman, Marcel Bich.
I'll have to wear it like a badge
of this scribbler's trade – alongside
the optional extra of nicotine
glazing my fingernails a tannin red –
fast-drying stuff, lightfast, semi-waterproof
(an anathema to the Chinese who judged
even bottled ink barbarian junk)
– black ink, heart's blood, mark of Cain.

But suppose that Abel was a Neanderthal
and Cain the Modern that killed him off,
less smiled on by God with his fenced settlements
and vegetable produce, but still
the one who went on to invent
biros, and write the myths of primal guilt
while the other was washed out from the gene pool
– him and his pointless stone-cobble tools,
his thick brow and pitted occipital
bulge and tender child burials, arrayed
with red deer teeth and red-ochred hide . . .
the first blood of fratricide
clotting the inkwell, crow quill or hollow reed
– sign of repentance, black bile, ox gall.

Chrome Yellow

Your three brave sunflowers are ready to drop.
Standing in a jug of stale drink
they've all about reached a steepening patch
on the curve of decay. Their dark-eyed
flameheads raddle at the tips and close,
then, lax as pulp or crape, they start to droop
on thick eyestalks. That mad Dutchman
who crammed his mouth with the chrome yellow
he used by the tubeful to paint them
made toxic lead his edible gold.
Their gold now lead, the sunflowers turn
towards the black sun of the earth.
Their time has gone. Their big leaves drape
and darken round them like a field of crows.

No Smoke without Fire

So ingrained by now are the lessons of safe sex
even in my dreams I wear a Durex

but afterwards still crave some finecut
bright Virginia shag and the delicate

friction of rice
or liquorice.

The Needful

The needful thing is missing from the day
but everyone proceeds as though it's fine
– like when we waited for the nightingale
and all we heard was the army firing range;

or when the bridegroom failed to find the ring,
fumbling in the shallows of his pockets
till the priest ventured an exchange in the wording:
without this ring I wed thee anyway;

or when the iron crown of Monza
with its one nail from the true cross
was not at hand for Henry's coronation
but in a pawnshop somewhere in Milan.

A Mole of Sorts

The digging creature has been at work again
out there – first a modest trough with a crest
of dry earth, fit for a starling or a thrush
to rest in. No big deal except to some yellow ants
doing repairs, carrying stuff on their hods.
Next day the hole was deeper,
deeper and wider, encroaching on the lawn
which yielded inch by inch each clump of turf
as though to a pendulum or scythe.

Asleep, I sat talking to an animal:
three, four foot long with silky white fur
and slim interminable fingernails
lucid as biro shafts or goose quills.
They made the plasticky click
of knitting needles as he waved them
in front of his pink snout as if to dry
the shining varnish. He was indeed,
he declared to me, a mole of sorts.

In a question of days, two weeks at most,
the lavender, the rose bush, the bay plant,
the bindweed, the lilac tree, the brambles
and the potato vine had disappeared,
leaving a long rectangular pit
like the foundations of a house
that would never be built, never be lived in.
Then I suppose that was the job done
and the digger moved on to another plot.

Obit.

The *magic vox*'s pale green disc
blinks like an airplane tail-light
or an astral event: a voice from *The Times*
is asking if I'd like to write
an obituary for Bertolucci
– the father, the poet, not the filmmaker.
Necrologue. 'Crocodile'. 'Obelisk'.
Which leaves a couple of days to bone up on
his life and works, to pry into his *Capanna
indiana* (shed or tepee?) and his *Camera da letto*
feeling like a rank outsider
who's intruded on a family funeral
or a paid mourner desirous everyone should know
how much the departed meant to him.

I remember him well in the cover photo
before that hilltop Parma village he was from
(whose name I've forgotten)
in a sadly festive, broad-brimmed hat
that shades his eyes. He called his condition
melancholia not depression, which made it sound
planetary rather than clinical.
Under the strain of obligation – of the 'required',
as opposed to what: the superfluous? the inspired? –
the more I read the less I understand,
the less I understand the more I warm
to the way his quiet voice is fretted
by 'the hopeless fatal transit of time',
the sense of loss that flowered from his hands.

Guide

Though sometimes she takes the industrially scenic route
canalside past the fiery furnace and the cryogenics factory

most days she leads the newly arrived
down the cobbled alleys of the old city

ignoring the Roman column the ditch the Saracen tower
even the corkscrew curls of Minos' tail

then with the ghost of a smile I've not forgotten
she leaves them at the edge with its balustrade

its kiosk selling sea-cool tentacles
deckchairs the stripes have faded from

and a coin-operated telescope trained
on the wide storm-terraces

where the luxurious spirits flock
whose desire is still so intense it sees in the total dark.

The Canary Principle

Port-end of Las Ramblas
where a cack-streaked Columbus
perched on his column
looks back to the New World,
the stacked birdcages house
canaries budgies parakeets macaws
while somehow got free
– word is their owners couldn't stand
such constant ugly noise –
the lime-green quaker parrots
make marrow-curdling crowlike caws
and short-stop flights from frond to frond.
In their thousands
they've colonised the palm trees in the plazas,
unfazed by the summer heat and
the now suspiciously mild winters
of this for them far northern latitude.

Your teacher the flautist Salvador Gratacós
chose a star canary to take home
where to his delight it kept abreast
of his practice trills and semi-quavers,
seeding them with ornamental riffs and curlicues
till one day the bird stopped dead mid-song,
disconsolate, surpassed, and wouldn't add
another phrase. Its syrinx locked.
At the stall they explained that once outsung
it never sings again. With the next: the same,
and so on till his room was filled with rows
of lemon-yellow mute canaries
that pecked at their plastic mirrors or honed

their dumb beaks on cuttlebones,
eyeing the maestro's
slightly spatulate fingertips
flying over the silver keys and stops.

Nave del Lagarto, Seville

The Sultan
of Egypt sent
Alfonso X jewels,
cloths, medicinal herbs,
a giraffe and a large crocodile
as a dowry for the king's daughter.
The gifts were returned all except for
the animals. When the crocodile died
it was cured, stuffed with straw, secured
above the gate to the Court of Orange-Trees.

For five
hundred years
it suffered innumerable
loving restorations – all listed
with the names of the artisans
on a parchment found between its jaws
– varnished, lacquered, glued, till too far gone,
in 1752, it was supplanted by a wooden sculpture.

Within
three years
shock waves
from the Lisbon
earthquake loosed
a stone from the Giralda
that crushed it. A new crocodile,
Crocodile III, still hangs there with a
prepared speech sealed in its mouth like
the best man at a wedding that was not to be.

Polonius

When his students smirked and agreed Polonius
was an old fool, Berryman challenged them
to frame some advice of their own as sound
as that parting speech to Laertes.
He got mad at them, I guess, for being so wise
they were stupid, for being themselves willing
to stab the old man in the arras,
for feeling themselves, like Hamlet, above judgement,
for thinking a corpse, whoever's corpse, meant nothing.
'This above all to thine own self be true'

is fine as far as it goes but it posits
a self as something essentially good;
whereas being true to a certain kind of self
could mean only damage to others,
but then Polonius might say to me that's not the true self
but a false one there's no point in being true to.
I sometimes find myself on the verge
of giving advice but then the words come out wrong
and all I've said is 'It's hard to know what's best'
or I breathe deep and the air stays stuck in my lungs.

On the eve of departure the two things
his father told my father not to do
were wear a wig or join the Masons
– being himself a Mason, and wearing a wig.
They'd come to weigh upon his conscience,
these two secrets that having once assumed
he found all but impossible to discard.
The advice is impeccable: No Masonry. No Wigs.
He might have added 'And No Hard Liquor'
but that was a problem he was still immersed in.

For years he carried a revolver
hidden about his person, having received
a number of anonymous death threats
– *he* wasn't going to be stabbed without a struggle –
but late one evening alone on the ferry
finally he threw the thing into the Mersey.
I think of it lying there under the tides,
a dead weight of potential energy,
with a flattened bubble of air – like a thought
that has yet to surface – trapped in its barrel.

Unfaded

The dead are villains we pretend to love.
Their waxy faces a serene reproach.
We learn their secrets with distaste:

the things they did make them at least
as bad as we are – even worse because
they're dead, and we're alive and might improve.

The dead are villains we pretend to love.
They died deliberately to spite us,
to leech our lifeblood for their awful dryness.

We clothe their faults in all the virtues
they never had, to keep them in their place,
where they should stay, away from us.

The dead are villains we pretend to love
though every now and then we hear their voice
speaking exactly as they spoke to us,

and see their smiles again as they once smiled,
and their hair unfaded as it was in life.

Twain

When I heard tonight how a man had dived
off a yacht and hit a passing turtle
and ended chairbound, I thought of your fatal
encounter with a pheasant.

Last night I rented *Gosford Park* on DVD:
the hunting party's leaving the big house
and one of them asks in a chirpy voice,
'I say, can pheasants be dangerous?'

Only for bikers, I found myself muttering.
Who could devise such meetings of the twain
– flesh versus horny scute, or startled wing –

could plot their course through empty air and ocean
till the final second, with this precision,
except a mad narrator, or an assassin?

Penal Architecture

*There are in London . . . notwithstanding we are a nation of liberty,
more publick and private prisons and houses of confinement, than
any city in Europe, perhaps as many as in all the capital cities of
Europe put together . . .*

Daniel Defoe, *A Tour through England and Wales*

*And of course the exterior was magnificent, even sublime – about
that all contemporary commentators were agreed. After its
completion they would also agree that it was a bad prison
from any other point of view. In particular the interior was
close, airless and insalubrious.*

Robin Evans, *The Fabrication of Virtue*

With a touch of excess or overkill,
George Dance the younger
had actual iron chains
pinned to the rusticated stone
on either side of the double door
of Newgate Gaol.

Drawing the pediment
he thought of Dante,
just a consonant away,
and Milton's gates of adamant.
He was after a kind of
sombre, frozen music,
a literal metaphor –
turning the flow of words
back into things.

The mind is its own place
and can stress
the lock not the hinge
in the idea of door.

Piranesi
(Carceri d'invenzione)

The thwarted architect has etched instead
the things he couldn't build – on such a scale
that nothing merely built could ever touch
the heights they reached. Monster stone had made

its masters antmen, miniatures who point
at vastness overhead or droop dead-spirited
on column stumps. Mountains of marble
bitten into copper: urns, temples, tombs,

obelisks and pyramids till from a surfeit
of stone his mind forged its own manacles
and hewed out gaols to dwarf the Pantheon

with winches, wrenching engines, spinal stairs
that, rising, endlessly invent new levels
where endlessness will offer no escape.

When Casement Crossed the Line

The great Pole for whom the British Empire
was a last ditch, a last line of defence
against darkness, even its own darkness,
even if finally a useless defence,
all stress-cracked rivets and spoiled engine rods
and bolstered by a necessary lie,
drew the line at treachery, and wouldn't send
a line to, let alone visit, his friend
in Brixton Gaol. Their fellowship
of horror at Leopold's Congo – at wounds,
weals and keloids from the rhino-hide whip,
at the dark, dry harvest of severed hands
laid out on duck-boards in forest stations
to line Europe's vaults with ivory
for its false teeth billiard balls piano keys
and in rubber plantations
to meet the demand for pneumatic tyres –
was now discounted. He'd simply cancelled himself
along with his consulships and knighthood,
along with his Commissioned Enquiry
into the Peruvian Amazon Co.
– its findings of maltreatment and murder
published in 1912 as a Blue Book.

The poet laureate, Alfred Noyes,
heedful of his master's voice,
spread rumours abroad about *The Black Diaries*:
'they touch the lowest depths of degradation'
though later (wrong again) he'd write his book
declaring them a forgery.
– Eyes agog at a strolling *cholo*'s penis:
'I [word illegible]'d (*rogered?*) him with Vaseline.'

'Also dark eyed lad who said *Buenas*
noches as he passed . . .'
Calls for the firing squad, the noose.
After years of witness for the dispossessed
he cut his last links with the possessors
and impaled himself on a principle.
Hopeless on the coast of Kerry, at Banna Strand,
near a small place called Curraghane
he landed in a collapsible curragh
mid-war, with two others, to fight for Ireland.
Him and whose army? Not the Kaiser's.
Not even that band of Gaels
he'd tried to recruit in German gaols,
his own mini-brigade, whose lives, unlike his own,
he was disinclined to put on the line.

Ès el senyor Gaudí!

Trapezoid headgear undulant
        the tram flashed and brushed
    Gaudí aside in the Carrer de Bailén
a stone's throw from his own Pedrera
   – that den for giant salamanders
(*un abri pour les dinosaurs*, Clemenceau
        called the Casa Milà)
lovingly curved out of malleable stone
from the torqued, betiled, cloud-bulbous chimney stacks
    to the dragonish ironwork balconies . . .
an architecture endlessly enjambed
       – broken-limbed,
his heart all but end-stopped, they brought him
    to and nursed him in
l'Hospital de la Santa Creu
     – a ward for paupers, seeing this tramp
        they didn't know from Adam
   (who, when they did, refused to be moved)
his pockets full of nothing but sunflower seeds
his head a quarry of unfinished projects:
   the troublesome parabolic vaults
      he meant
   for the velvet factory church,
a roofscape like a Moorish tent, another
    salamander (salaam & amen),
five bony, tilted, elephantine pillars
to bear the load of all he left behind.

Vocations

Rosary, pillar, garden, assumption, solitude:
the five Marías you and your sisters make,
distinguished by the vocations of the Virgin.

Amongst you all resemblance hides
in posture, gesture, hand or voice
like a vein of dusky mauve –

tint of the five figs that Frederic Amat,
the Catalan artist as a young man,
at home with colour and conjugations,

slyly portrayed the group of you as
– now hung among the oak-framed monochrome engravings
showing the Napoleonic light infantry

in a series of Peninsular engagements.
The others settled in Bilbao, Madrid, or stayed
within earshot of the calle Aragón,

and you – *por suerte* – here, still here
where the potted fig, its first fruits stricken,
makes the most of what light there is,

blue guest of the early frost.

The Napkin Lifter
(Catullus XII)

Marrucinus Asinius, your sinister manoeuvre –
letting your left hand hover over
a fellow diner's lap as he leans to hear
a punchline or pour wine
from a carafe – respects neither
the gods of wine nor conversation.
And what does it mean? It means I'm afraid
you're at your old trick of stealing napkins
– an act that isn't clever, nor even that skilful,
merely sad and graceless in my book. But why
believe me when you can go ask your brother
Pollio, a gifted, witty, really charming boy,
who'd gladly fork out coffers full of hush-money
to keep your vileness unremarked. So either
steel yourself for a several-hundred-liner
of relentless, barbed hendecasyllables
or send me back that lovely piece of linen.
And don't think I'm irked because it's worth so much:
memory is something other than a cash till –
the whole set of fine Valencian serviettes
was sent from distant Spain by Fabullus
and Veranius as a gift I'm therefore
bound to care for as I care
for Veranolo mio and for Fabullus.

The Resort

Red-eyed and flinching, Flavius
was applying a depilatory paste
of ivy gum and crushed centipede
to little effect. The sudden silence meant
they were waiting for that smooth-cheeked
decimvir to swivel his thumb
over in the arena. Brats of empire
– they'd think the world revolved around them
if they thought the world revolved
which of course it doesn't. It stays put
or gets worse, like this heat. A plague
of copulating crystal-winged flies

alights indifferently on plates of meat,
on fruit, on us – a sign of thunder or just
more heat. A sated roar comes from the stalls.
Wild beasts are all the rage in Rome
and here too we import somnolent crocodiles
that only strike when the prisoner's goaded
within three steps of their jaws;
and a great ape that can tear men apart.
My friend Smyntheus, aptly named
after the god of plagues, has had his walls
turned into an entire menagerie
by a Greek dauber with a taste for narrative.

But waiting for war all narrative
has forsaken us: as if these workouts
were reason enough for our existence
or at least provided one for strigils.
I claim the word's derived from stryx, the owl,
from the shape of the owl's claw, but Smyntheus
calls that spurious etymology and says

the two words are unrelated and the only
animals involved at all are bees
which have barbed legs to clean their antennae.
Basted in oil and sweat, we think our health
may be all the claws and antennae we need.

Obelisk

There are certain houses built
  not to be lived in – long
houses pyramids and this
  the Axum Obelisk
that stood nearly seventy years
  an exiled axle
near the Circus Maximus
  whilst at its home in the Horn
a site's been dug a pit a pause
  a prolonged hiatus
that mortal span's an eyeblink
  in its career made
to measure and memorialise
  deep time a dial
for solar or for astral time –
  solo un attimo
but children now grown old
  remember its removal
when thinking like a Roman
  Dux Mussolini spoke
have it shipped to Rome
  to celebrate a victory
won by poison gas
  re-erecting its five
fallen pieces each almost
  unbudgeable the whole
some hundred and forty tons
  – cut with helicoidal wire
those same dismantled blocks
  still wait for their return
in a Fiumicino warehouse
  an airport longhouse

on the first available US
    Galaxy plane
certain houses have no space
    inside for living
though some like this are fitted
    with doors front and back
and windows which won't open
    rock-solid granite
that waits on us and fathoms space
    but now it's time high time
this long house went home

Black Gold

Here are the Carthaginian figs – Ciano
grinned as he handed Mussolini
some specimen chunk of shiny
copper ore from the Lezhë mine
in conquered Albania.

And here are the figs of Mesopotamia –
Vice President Cheney
traces on the map the red-marked pipeline
from the fields of Rumaila and Kirkuk
to the Turkish port of Ceyhan.

Black Mountain (1933)

It should be clear by now that our way of studying colour does not start with the past – neither with works of the past nor with its theories . . . Thus we replace looking backward by looking first at ourselves and our surroundings, and replace retrospection with introspection.

Josef Albers, *Interaction with Colour*

Out walking in pastures new,
in the first months of exile, Anni Albers
– by a shade the better linguist –
was teaching her husband English

when he asked her
what pasture meant
and she replied: *Das ist klar*:
the opposite of future.

He has a mind not to graze on
that type of pasture
(his fields of stained, reticulated glass)
whilst the future was square,
an endless choir and afterlife of squares
in razor-contoured oil on masonite.

In the Year of the Blue Angel

Hybrid, heterotactic, Hannah Höch
has made an obelisk of Marlene's legs,
her high, her *höchlich*, heels
kicked heavenward, her thighs
mounted on a pilaster and plinth
with the deftest of joins. Cuts
and joints are how she dwells upon
and realigns the broken world, the cut-
and-thrust of cut-and-paste: sewing-patterns
for the future's shirt; ethnographical haute couture.
Hovering, spliced and grafted, who's that
coleopterous lady in a state
of unavailing angst? – X marks the four
dragonfly wings, the entrechat
of Höch's scissors as they clip and cut
such naked lengths of everything.
Oils, owls, ills and all else
made well. Never bored or blunted.
So how did a
good quiet girl from Gotha,
Hans Richter belittlingly
wondered, get mixed up
in the big unruly world of Dada? With
ease – uneasily she mixed the media,
sexes, species. Mixed maximum with microbe.
Her answer to a Nazi art-group
weirdly wanting her to join them, if,
that is, she had no Jewish blood
was a curt
Nein!

Her friends had gone
but what remained was ink oil cut-
outs magazines and watercolours not
so much blended as abutted and upended.

An Encroachment

Now I can take over your side of the bed
I discover the little space between
the bedside and the wall I'd been
unaware of – where you'd made

an installation like a survival kit:
biros specs nailfiles novels magazines
tubes of mild medicaments and creams
one decorative box with nothing in it.

I lift the nothing out and stare at it.
Never has nothing looked more splendid.
Fearful I've left a smudge and marred it
I quickly put it back and shut the lid.

Meeting of Minds

When we meet, me and my neighbour Michael,
we tend to agree
we'd like to strangle someone.

Who that is depends. I for instance
might have in mind a certain person
and he an alternative but we listen
to each other, deferring
to the other's grievance, the facts of each case.

There's no telling how far the blame extends
– we both know full well it does extend
far down the road and back in time and way beyond
the bounds we've set – but in fairness
we find it helps to keep the numbers down

and not to overreach ourselves. But then his dog
has had enough of what, in his little world,
he probably thinks of as just standing still
and makes a series of resentful tugs
braced at the leash until, behind his back,

my neighbour rolls his eyes and I agree
with a nod. Must be off,
he sighs and me: Right see you soon then Mick.

Ire

Not for a moment was the real wasp fooled
by the fake wasp's black-and-yellow costume:
instead of being flattered or amused,
she seized the hover fly and stung its face
while her jaws hacksawed through its torso.
In that embrace you could clearly see
how such clever jewelled mimicry,
all jasper and jet, was several shades astray,
too beetle-bright and ultimately pointless.
But so much deadly ire at imitation!
The counterfeiter pulsed its flimsy wings
so the wasp tore them out and let them fall
then flew off with the rest of her disciple
to whisper in its ear one final lesson.

Typtography
for Valerio Magrelli

A monarchic silence as of the grave
reigned in the Peter and Paul Fortress
where Peter had tortured and killed his son Alexis.

The felted floors and walls would answer nothing
to Kropotkin's knocking. He exercised his arms
with the wooden stool and walked seven versts each day

up and down the cell. On the small oak table
he wrote *The Glacial Period and Orography of Asia*
when that vindictive Romanov, Alexander II,

finally conceded him pen and ink – 'just till sunset'.
Which occurred at two o'clock in winter.
Summer 1875, after the mass arrests, the silence broke

and a series of taps spelt out KTO VY?
(Who are you?) His friend Surdokov, as it happened,
and a peasant, below, who lost his mind.

The Cyrillic alphabet was broken down
into six rows of five letters, which made
conversation slightly less laborious.

Moved to the House of Detention,
weaker now so he could barely lift the stool,
but one step nearer his glorious escape,

he narrated to the young man in the next cell
the history of the Paris Commune
which took, however, a whole week of tapping.

The Book of Names

There's a man going round taking names . . .

Between Termini and a few stops back
some fetid little cutpurse took a blade

to my leather shoulder bag behind my back,
slipped his deft paw in and helped himself

to the address book he most likely felt
was my wallet. And now he has the names

of my friends in the palm of his hand.
Will he ring them or write? – Arrange to meet

at the caffè under the Rotonda
where soon enough my presence won't be missed

and he'll win his way into their tenderest
considerations with his gambler's charm, easily

overstepping the mark I'd always failed to,
while I sit on a bench and watch the sun

nose into the gashed bag and bring to light
its sad and evil remnants deemed not fit

to lift, with the one thought
of where I'd find a cobbler's needle

and some right-coloured thread to mend the cut
to cover up the shame, the sudden lightness.

from
OUT THERE

Out There

If space begins at an indefinite zone
where the chance of two gas molecules colliding
is rarer than a green dog or a blue moon
then that's as near as we can get to nothing.

Nostalgia for the earth and its atmosphere
weakens the flesh and bones of cosmonauts.
One woke to find his crewmate in a space suit
and asked where he was going. For a walk.

He had to sleep between him and the air-lock.
Another heard a dog bark and a child cry
halfway to the moon. What once had been

where heaven was is barren beyond imagining,
and never so keenly as from out there can
the lost feel earth's the only paradise.

On Nothing

*I do not think it is absurd for you to say that nothing is something,
since no one can deny that 'nothing' is a noun.*

Anselm of Canterbury

If nothing is the opposite of something
then it too is something and not nothing.
Or is that just language rushing in
to fill what makes the intellect recoil?

It's us, not nature, that abhors a vacuum,
for in frictionless space there's still a fraction
more than nothing, if not enough of it
to slow the planets in their orbits.

But the full moon hides its emptiness
and every plenitude its opposite;
the present buckles into nowlessness

that lasts for never as a dark star draws
downward threads of light. There nothing exists,
couching like a sphinx among the rubble.

The Perils

Think of the perils of seafarers and the perils of travellers by
land! Anyone walking anywhere is liable to sudden accidents . . .
One would suppose the sitting posture to be perfectly safe.
And yet . . .
  St Augustine, *The City of God*

We may be wise enough to shun the waves
but only folly would suppose
the land is safe: land is deeper than the sea.
Rock, sand and soil all have their perils.

Quakes raze and floods submerge our habitations.
One bite from a rabid dog makes man feared
by his own family as much as any
wild beast. The body itself is heir to

more foul diseases than the books
of physicians can accommodate.
Walking anywhere is constant danger.

Even seated at my desk to write this
I remember the priest Eli who fell
from his chair never to rise again.

A Safe Distance

If the moon were closer, quite apart
from disasters it would wreak on earth,
how soon before that chiaroscuro,
the light-splashed pores and shadowy pits,
engrossing so much of the night sky
and dimming half the constellations,
would start to pall? By the same rule
the distance that divides us seems
providentially assigned so that
from here you still look radiant, majestic.

Après

When the flood waters left they left
the pine boards cupped; the plaster blistered
with salts; the cheap chipboard
bursting out of its laminate jacket
in all the kitchen units; the electrics wrecked
with the wires firing in the sockets;
the polyfilled cracks in the buckled doors
once more agape; the iron grate sporting
a hem of rust and the ash it contained
arranged in a scum-line above the skirting;
dampness, months deep, fattening the pores
of the brickwork; a question mark over the slate floor;
the oven fouled; the fridge unsafe; the whole place
humming with marsh rot and fetor
but the garden, the garden good, and greener
for an alien crop of hogweed higher
than us, hardy, sturdy, hirsute, armed
with a poison sap against expulsion.

Teazles

Out in the vacant lot to gather weeds
I found these teazles – their ovoid heads
delicately armoured with crowns of thorns.
Arthur, from whom I haven't heard a word
in thirty years, who must be ninety if
he's a day, told me they were used to raise
the nap on the green felt of billiards tables
and, since Roman times, for combing woollen stuff.
He also said their seeds were caviar
to the goldfinch. And then I lost the knife
he'd lent me to cut some – the loss of which
was the cause of grief. In honour of gruff Arthur
I shake the seeds out in our small green patch
and stick the spiky seed heads in a jar.

Bark

A tour of all the trees that grow
in Barcelona's port was my reward
for buzzing, uninvited, at María's door.
She knew each one by name and character:
oleander, tamarind, the four or five
orders of palm, Corinthian-topped or
plain Ionic. But the *palo borracho*
was unlike anything I'd seen before:
its every inch of bark a skewering spike
worse than a bite: horrid, arid, hard
as nails, leaving nothing unprotected
but a few pink flowers. Ogre-like, unlike
us, who harden grimmer year by year,
with age it sheds the armour that it wore.

Oak

When my father saw an advert in the *Echo*
for a big house at a peppercorn rent
he rang and heard a voice with a slight croak
enquire – Can you read a map? – Yes. – OK
meet me tomorrow noon . . . (the voice gave co-ordinates).
So he drove through the green deep past Wenlock
and stopped in a lane beside a field gate
where soon another car appeared
and unburdened itself of an elderly gent.
– The name's Forester. (Eliding the Lord.)
He walked my father to the gate and asked
what he could see: at first, nothing but trees
in the distance. – D'you mean *that* . . . magnificent oak?
– The house is yours. I'll have them send the keys.

The Gate

This sawn-off backdoor has become a gate,
nicely fitting a gap in the fence.
Unlike the door it was, the gate keeps
nothing out: not the creatures of jet and agate
nor the toads and newts that shuffle under
its ragged footrail. Least of all the flood that overflows
the reservoir and breaches all defences.
The gate unites the space it splits asunder
and lets you in to/out of, more or less
the same thing, joining green to green, earth

to earth: same light, same weather either side.
A superfluous barrier: openness
traverses it. Unbounded air ignores
the interruption. More art than function,
even if my neighbour, pointing at the paint
I half scraped off, just sees an eyesore.
As yet it yields to the slightest pressure,
but in time it may define a frontier, once more
divide the outside from the inside.
The door again, but of a redimensioned house.

First and Last

Effect preceded cause: the storm
conjured the butterfly's wing, a dusky,

spattered wing, with a black quoit
afloat on a red ground; and the blasted oak

called forth the skittish thunderbolt;
and the earthquake that shook a city off

the earth's back had already tampered with
the continental plates; and the tremor I felt

when your face appeared made your face appear
a flawless catastrophe, prime mover and last word.

I fell, but the fall preceded that first sight.

Epithets

Toledo la rica, Salamanca la fuerte, Leon la bella,
Oviedo la sacra, y Sevilla la grande.

Liverpool the impoverished, the liverish, the void, the full,
the self-besotted, the blarney-argoted, the blitzed and
    blackened,
the *bella-brutta*, the rag-rich, the moss-stained sandstoned,
the green-lung'd, the ricket-ridden, the loud and adenoidal.

Liverpool the last-to-be-served, the least-accounted,
the over-arched and undermined, the mother-tongued and
    plurilingual,
the Catholic-Protestant, the cap-in-hand, the hand-
to-mouth, the pub-encrusted and the hovel-haunted.

Liverpool the riverine, the ocean-avid, the slaveship-tainted,
sugar-whitening, matchstick-making, slum and dockland
refuge of Lascars, Chinese, Irish, Jews, Somalians.

Liverpool the deserted, the polluted, the *de bon aire*,
the clinker-built and shipwrecked, the chameleon,
the edge-of-everywhere-and-nowhere's-centre.

El Puente de los Peligros, Murcia
for Mick Imlah

By the Bridge of Perils we looked down on the Segura,
'one of the most polluted rivers in Europe',
though safe enough for a colony of tortoises,
arrived from Africa, to be basking on a mud bank.

The day's task: to translate 'La Luna' by Borges,
and we were skiving off. I quoted mine
called 'Mooning' which shed a whole new light
on the final line: *¡Mírala! Es tu espejo.*

It won a smile. You were handsome as a Roman tortoise
as Lorca said of the Gaditan singer Ignacio Espeleta,
and no more than him inclined to work – within a day, the
     pretty
festival assistants had set their hearts on you.

But all the same, against the grain, you did work,
you did the work which overtook the hares
at the last curve – you couldn't have left it later
for *The Lost Leader* to nonchalantly lead the field.

Of course it's not a race or competition, and sport
always seemed to me the opposite of poems but for you
it's like they had a common source in speed, panache,
the human stripped of all accoutrements and props

facing its limits. I miss – word that does what it says –
those *cervezas* under the cathedral's
clashing Gothic and Baroque. I miss your swarthy Caledonian
duende, the deadpan pranks, the glinting wit,

your judgement's slow sure coil and lightning-quick release.

Ethics & Aesthetics

When Franco had Aranguren
the Professor of Ethics
in Madrid
fired
for his involvement in student politics

Barcelona's Professor of Aesthetics
the poet Valverde
resigned with a note that read
nulla aesthetica sine ethica

– gesture and word so wed
they twisted an *Either/Or*
into a well-knotted
ampersand

and fastened a rope bridge across a chasm

The Deadhouse

Somerset House

Ooliths in a Jurassic bath of micrite:
the palatial, weathered white of Portland stone.
I too would prefer to watch the work of masons

than hear sermons. Watch them mallet down
the granite paving cubes, dress limestone,
engrave the slab of the Queen's Lady-in-Waiting:

CY GIST LE CORPS DE DEFVNCTE CATHERINE
GVILERMET. PRIEZ DIEV POVR SON AME.

*

Catchpool of sound in the sheer lightwell.
Catchpool of light in the deep soundwell.
A faint swell of water at the palace roots.

Ting-tang, the quarter chimes from the birdcage
cast frame in the West Wing, clockwork
by Vulliamy. Its silent fellow in the East.

The rivergate now a sweeping arch left on
the stone manuscript. Bricked in, the river embanked.

*

Creases of thick water, iron-filed and polished.
Silken rucks as the river eases and edges past
the bridge, glistened, scuffed and scored like a zinc plate

half-cleared of ink. Fiddleheads of swirls,
fishtail eddies. Its own level. Sea level.
Rolled up seacharts like telescopes

in the Navy Board storeroom.
The thrumming engine of empire.

*

Mind-forged, unreal city. The weight
of stone on each square foot of earth.
At least the river is its own weight, give or take

the passing traffic. Makes a silvery tear
where the light floods in, pools in the soundwell.
Scaresome the outreach of its administrations,

the intent skulking in its bridges' shadows, its
tentacular, inky dusk with fishlamps scowling.

*

Loath to be lured to the glove of the falconer
with a strip of bush-meat, the Harris hawk,
employed to chase pigeons from the Deadhouse,

perches on a lagged pipe, settles its gold tail-feathers
and glares at the tombstone of the king's priest.
Upstairs the taxes rendered unto Caesar

his own minted image or hologram,
while the river, withdrawn to a new margin,
reflects gold glass from the wavering,

hollow towers of commerce where the profiteers
long for their 'strong and stable government'.
The skaters wait till winter for their rink.

The Fly Inventory

The fly by night.
The fly in the ointment.
The fly in amber.
The fly on the wall.
The fly on the wall
in Petrus Christus's *Portrait of a Carthusian*
often considered a *memento mori*
though it could be a demonic distraction from prayer.
Or a model of seraphic stillness.
Holub's fly at the Battle of Crécy.
The five kinds of fly I counted today
on a single umbel of the yarrow
including a greenbottle,
with crimson headlights and cupreous bodywork,
avidly hoovering pollen
through a black trumpet thicker than its legs.
The black-and-white human fly by Luc Tuymans
undergoing a sinister metamorphosis.
The fly in the film *The Fly*.
The fly in the remake *The Fly*.
The fly on the frieze in the *mercato di lana* at Pompeii.
The fly that bit the flying horse that caused the fall
of Bellerophon into a thorn bush.
The fly without teeth
but a copious supply of saliva.
The fly in the coal-shed that Mahon
set beside the *Winged Victory of Samothrace*,
so braced against each other it's hard to know
which of them he thought up first.
The flies of Machado, Blake and Dickinson.
But that's enough fly poems
though there's also 'the marble fly': Mandelstam's nickname.

The fly's stealthy ovipositor
that prises open a dead linnet's beak
under the patient eye of Jean Henri Fabre.
Una mosca muerta: used of someone not especially bright.
The fly on the pedestal not yet constructed
in the *plaza major* of the city of flies.
Beelzebub, the lord of the flies.
The fly within, the inner fly.
The fly that flew from the list of flies.
The fly that stops its din when you switch the light off
but starts again at dawn, and needs to check
whether you're still among the quick or dead.
The fly whisk; the fly swatter; fly spray;
the Fully Guaranteed Electric Fly Killer
– escalations in the war against the fly.
The fly that survived.

Guilt

Last night asleep I killed a poet
and nothing I did could resurrect him.
The shopping mall's defibrillator kit

was useless, and I drew the line at mouth-to-mouth.
Awake, the guilt remained – although he wasn't
even a good poet. Well, to be fair, there are worse.

I'd never had the least intent to harm him
unless an involuntary expression of disdain
and the absence of a single word of praise

makes one a murderer. It's not as though
his talents have gone unsung – sung they've been,
by a choir of critics. If I were to say

what irks me especially in his work,
he could put a name, his own name, to this:
he'd know it was him that I'd killed, and me

that had killed him, and then I'd have only
added insult to mortal injury.
It should ease my mind that there's no body,

no cordoned crime site, no chalk outline,
no weapon, no discernible motive.
But there it is: his blood is on my hands.

Stricken Proverbs

A full vessel is inaudible.

*

Every cliff has a glass edge,
every chasm a covering cloud.
Every lining has a hidden needle.

*

Many a sickle rakes the stubble.

*

A rip in space needs a stitch in time.

*

Time's flies wait to feast on no man.

*

Art longs for the brevity of life.

*

Never a nail in the blacksmith's forge,
nor a pen in the poet's pocket.

*

Home is where the heart can't live.

*

All Rome leads to are roads.

*

For the deep well: a long cord and a light bucket.

*

Where there's a will, there's a wall.

The Carved Buddha

Within the lotus bud of sandalwood that needs
to be pried open by a thumbnail the Buddha sits
cross-legged on a flower exuding the odour of resin
under a light coating of gold leaf.

It belonged to Mrs Ogilvie from Aberdeen:
when she opened the perfect fit of the upper lid
I knew that nothing made by the hand of man
could hold a candle to it. Its beauty blazed

but quietly, a tiny inexhaustible thing.
I instantly forgot the ban on brazen
idols, and remembered the mustard seed.

You could not guess what the small plain
capsule concealed, and when you saw
you guessed another light burnt from within.

The Meeting House

We have come to listen to the silence,
but the silence listens back at us.
Sparks in the blaze of its galactic dark,
we sit in a square that should have been a circle,

facing the oak table's bowl of oak leaves,
the Holy Bible overgrown with bark.
From the east window a sunbeam angles
down a ladder for the mute choir

of dust motes, or mites, or dancing atoms,
but no one breaks the silence which is made
from the base upwards like a bowl of clay,
as moments lapse into millennia

and minutes round into an hour. Then one
of the carved elders comes alive and shakes
his neighbour's hand: the room erupts in wood notes
as though a ladder's rungs were being strummed.

The Literalist

When told they'd be made into fishers of men
did it not occur to a single one
that he'd be best off staying a fisher of fish,

reluctant to catch men with the lure of heaven
 – an electric-blue dragonfly threaded
on an iron hook? That he'd no heart to land

shoals of men ashore to breathe the wrong air,
or have them kneel before a statue's crimson tears
operated by a small pump in the vestry?

That he wanted fish to be fish, and not multiplied
ad infinitum by unearthliness;
wanted loaves to be loaves, salt waves to be waves

and not a secret floor the saviour walks on?
Just to sink when he sank and swim when he swam.